A Heartbeat from Eternity

Lessons Learned Before, During, and After My Journey to Eternity

By: Gail Leaphart

Leaping Heart Press
P. O. Box 41803, Fayetteville, NC 28309-1803

First printing: October 2017

Leaping Heart Press, P. O. Box 41803, Fayetteville, NC 28309-1803

Scripture marked *KJV* are taken from the King James Version of the Bible.

Scripture marked *NKJV* are taken from the New King James Version®. Copyright © 1982 by Thomas Nelson. Used by permission. All rights reserved.

Scripture quotations marked (NIV) are taken from the Holy Bible, New International Version®, NIV®. Copyright © 1973, 1978, 1984, 2011 by Biblica, Inc.™ Used by permission of Zondervan. All rights reserved worldwide.

Scripture marked *MSG* are taken from The Message. Copyright © 1993, 1994, 1995, 1996, 2000, 2001, 2002. Used by permission of NavPress Publishing Group.

ISBN- 13: 978-1-948005-01-2

Please visit website for other forthcoming publications:

www.gailleaphart.com

For information regarding author interviews, please leave contact information on above website.

DEDICATION

I dedicate this book with gratitude and humility to my Lord and Savior, Jesus Christ, Who never gave up on me and rescued me from myself, my sin, and my enemy. I am completely overwhelmed by Your unconditional love for this former sinner saved by Grace!

Many thanks to those many precious prayer warriors and intercessors who never stopped believing and kept pounding the doors of heaven on my behalf when all hope seemed gone. You know who you are and God does too!

Much appreciation to the team of doctors, nurses, and staff of Pitt Memorial Hospital (now Vidant Medical Center) and Physicians East who provided me with the best medical care and attention to help sustain every bodily function until God's miraculous work was completed. May God bless each of you!

Thank you, Mary Tuley, for your patience, training, and editing of my first publication. I could never have done it without you!

A Heartbeat from Eternity

TABLE OF CONTENTS

Lesson 12   Reason for A MIRACLE!!!

The Sinner's Prayer – A Fresh Start!!!

INTRODUCTION

As I sit here writing this introduction to a story I know that many may doubt, some will discount, but hopefully, many will be touched and transformed by for eternity, I am humbled and honored to have the opportunity to give my Lord and Savior, Jesus Christ, all the glory and credit for an undeniable miracle. I am in total and complete awe of Him, but even more amazed that He would choose someone like me to share with you a true story of His unlimited power and never-ending love for us.

We have all heard the Bible stories of God using ordinary people to carry out His extraordinary plan, but believe me, I never even dreamed that God would use a little country bumpkin nobody like me to be a witness to many of His power and might. You see, by the world's standards I am a nobody (not rich, not famous, not a movie star, not a politician, not a beauty queen, not a college graduate, not even a lifelong follower of Jesus, and equipped with slow articulators causing a southern drawl that cannot be disguised), but thank God He specializes in using the things the world considers foolish, weak, or lacking to fulfill His purposes. 1 Corinthians 1:27 (NKJV) says it this way:

27 But God has chosen the foolish things of the world to put to shame the wise, and God has chosen the weak things of the world to put to shame the things which are mighty;

My hope is that you will understand that if He can save and use someone like me, He can and will save and use you too. There is no higher calling in life than to be used by God to help change the eternal destiny of another. My earnest prayer is that this book will cause you to stop and consider where you stand, not just in this life on earth, but for eternity. Give Jesus a chance to give you a brand new life, a fresh start, a do-over. He will forgive every sin you have committed (no matter how terrible), erase it as if you never did it, and then give you a purpose greater than yourself that will turn your dreams into reality. Submit your life to Him, develop a servant attitude, and the sky truly is the limit (no heavenly pun intended).

I also hope that everyone who reads this book will realize that God does not respect or show favoritism, He simply has a unique plan and purpose for each of us. The gift of salvation and life eternal in Heaven is available to everyone who simply accepts God's Son, Jesus Christ, as their Lord and Savior as explained in Romans 10:9-10 (NIV) which says:

9 If you declare with your mouth, "Jesus is Lord," and believe in your heart that God raised him from the dead, you will be saved. 10 For it is with your heart that you believe and are justified, and it is with your mouth that you profess your faith and are saved.

Once you receive this gift and make the decision to serve as an ambassador for the Kingdom of God, get ready for a great adventure. There is no greater honor than to serve the God Who created heaven and earth, no limit on where He might lead you, no door that He cannot open for a willing participant, and no higher calling in life than to help fulfill the ultimate goal of the Lord's Prayer stated in Matthew 6:10(KJV):

"Thy kingdom come, Thy will be done in earth, as it is in heaven."

You cannot imagine or fathom what God has in mind for you. Remove the limitations you have put on God and allow His greatness and majesty to work in your life. Get excited and let the adventure begin!

Don't wait, don't delay in making the most important decision in your life because, whether you believe it or not, you are always only *A Heartbeat From Eternity*! None of us knows when our heart will stop beating and we will have no time to make that decision. Whether you believe it or not, the Word of God tells us there is life after this life and everyone has the freewill to determine where they will spend it – heaven or hell! Many people think they are just too intelligent to believe this or they simply have been deceived by the lies of the enemy into doubting that the Word of God is really the Word of God. I would simply ask you a few questions: what if you are wrong? Have you ever been wrong about something you were once so sure of? Can you prove you are right? Are you willing to take that risk?

Get ready to read a true story that I pray will help you answer the question: where and how will you spend forever? Forever is a long time….but it's truly your choice!

Lesson One

A MESS!!!

My journey to eternity and back began in July 2000 when I learned during a regular yearly checkup that I had a small fibroid tumor. The gynecologist who was supposedly looking out for my health at that time (and who is no longer practicing medicine) acted as if the diagnosis was nothing. She told me that many women have fibroid tumors, the majority of which are benign and serve as the body's way of storing estrogen before menopause. However, I heard almost none of the explanation because my mind was focused on the word TUMOR!

I left the doctor's office in shock, with much concern and wondering what to do about this situation. After a sleepless night, I called the clinic to make an emergency appointment with the same gynecologist, hoping to gain some insight. When I met with her, though, she responded to me coldly, and in a flippant manner, reiterating that no further treatment would be necessary. She would simply monitor the tumor each year for changes. If I should experience any pain, discomfort, or unusual symptoms, I was to call for another appointment. My deep anxiety was rewarded with the equivalent of a great big yawn.

During the next year my only "symptom," which I did not associate with the tumor, was an expanding abdomen. I was exercising, eating right, and trying to control the change, but to no avail. Then when I returned to the gynecologist for my yearly checkup in June 2001, she was visibly shocked when she examined me and saw the unexpected growth of this tumor. Noting that it had tripled in bulk, to about the size of a small melon, she explained that my body was preparing for menopause, which would probably begin very soon. Again, I pressed her for information about possible treatment, and again she "assured" me that nothing needed to be done.

From June to November, my abdomen continued to expand, and I was soon unable to wear any article of clothing with a fitted waist – but thank God for the Internet! Since I felt compelled to rely on myself, I began going online to research treatments for fibroid tumors and complications associated with them. Unfortunately, the available information was limited and included only two recommended treatments: a complete hysterectomy, or a fairly new possibility known as a Uterine Artery Embolization (UAE). Why had my doctor never mentioned UAE to me? Had she hesitated because the UAE procedure is performed by a radiologist rather than a gynecologist – or was her reason devious, or even spiritual?

In November 2001, looking six months pregnant, I made another appointment, but this time I was armed with information about possible treatment. I told my doctor that I would like to pursue the UAE, since a complete hysterectomy could lead to hormone replacement therapy, an avenue that I hoped to avoid because there was a history of breast cancer in my family. Amazingly, my questions and concerns received a calloused and agitated response from this physician, who still insisted that I needed no treatment. However, if I wanted something done, I should consider a complete hysterectomy. Amazing! Because of the tumor's size, it would necessitate a rather large abdominal incision and a recovery period of at least eight weeks. I had been seeking help for twenty months!

When I informed the doctor that I was interested in the UAE procedure and wanted to determine whether I was a likely candidate for it, she first resisted. Nevertheless, I replied that, if she would not refer me to a qualified radiologist familiar with the UAE, I would find a gynecologist who would. She then reluctantly named a local radiologist who had already completed twelve successful UAE procedures.

In early December 2001, I was examined to determine my compatibility with the UAE. Once I received a favorable report, the radiologist informed me that he would submit the pertinent information, including my gynecologist's input, to my insurance company. In late January, unfortunately, my request for the UAE was denied because it was considered "an experimental procedure." The next step was an appeal from my two doctors and me, and this letter included additional supporting information specifying why I needed the procedure. After waiting several weeks, though, I received a second denial from my insurance company, this one asserting that, even though hundreds of UAE procedures had been performed successfully across the United States, the concept was still considered experimental.

In March 2001, I received a third denial! We had submitted our second appeal to the insurance company, including additional information supporting the procedure in general, testimonials from several of my radiologist's patients who had undergone the UAE procedure, and some very impressive success rates. So I was stunned, and the radiologist was surprised as well – but neither of us realized that the gynecologist was undermining my request by providing the insurance company with little or no support of the procedure.

In April 2002, while working on my third appeal to the insurance company, I returned to the gynecologist's office for a checkup and found her reaction agitated. Obviously, she opposed my decision to proceed with trying to have the UAE, and I finally decided to ask her about her beliefs. Shouldn't she, as my doctor, want what was best for me? Why should my decision upset her? Shouldn't I be able to pursue any legal treatment that might forestall a more invasive operation?

After several tense minutes, I sought permission to ask her a personal question, and she commented, "You can ask. I'm not sure I will answer." She may have imagined that I would ask what she might do if she were in my shoes, but instead I asked, "Are you a Christian?" Almost like the possessed girl in *The Exorcist* whose head twisted around, she shouted furiously, "No, I am not! What does that have to do with this situation?"

"I now understand," I said, "why you truly don't have my best interests at heart. You are no longer my doctor." Then I left her office and never returned. Instead, I called the office of a gynecologist who attended our church and made an appointment with him, Before I could meet with him, though, I was admitted to the hospital. I was in a medical mess, but little did I know how serious a mess it was!

LESSON ONE: CHOOSE A CHRISTIAN DOCTOR IF AT ALL POSSIBLE! AND, IF EVER IN DOUBT, GET A SECOND OPINION...QUICKLY!

Lesson Two

My Test!!!

In the couple of years prior to 2002, I had grown in my walk with the Lord, and my faith in Him had strengthened tremendously. He was graciously preparing me when I wasn't even aware.

I was attending a church where the presence of the Holy Spirit was welcome, active, and apparent. While I read and studied the Word of God in my private time and attended weekly Bible studies led by some strong, Spirit-filled, mature Christian women, my faith in God and His Word soared! As Romans 10:17 (NKJV) says, ***"So then faith comes by hearing, and hearing by the word of God."***

Faith truly does come by hearing and hearing and hearing and **hearing by the Word of God.** We can never hear God's Word too much, and I now know that God had strengthened my faith through church and reading and Bible studies until I truly believed **every** syllable of The Word! I believed that God's desire was to heal me and that my healing was His will! I believed that He could and would speak to me and that I was ready to listen! As I look back on that amazing time, however, I realize that we never stop growing in our relationship with God and through the knowledge that He reveals to us through His Living Word. I know that my growth had only just begun because I had not yet received the baptism of the Holy Spirit!

"Then I remembered the word of the Lord, how He said, 'John indeed baptized with water, but you shall be baptized with the Holy Spirit'" (Acts 11:16, NKJV).

The morning after the radiologist declared me a valid candidate for the UAE, I was awakened at 4:32 by the Holy Spirit. I remember looking at the clock and wondering if I was dreaming that someone had called my name. In my spirit, though, I heard Him tell me to go into the family room, turn on the light, and listen, so of course I did. As I sat patiently on the sofa, my heartbeat accompanied only by the ticking of the wall clock, I clearly heard the voice of the Lord saying, "You will not have this procedure. I will heal you." Thrilled and rejoicing, I was completely convinced that I was healed and would require no procedure!

"Thus also faith by itself, if it does not have works, is dead" (James 2:17, NJKV).

At that point I had a decision to make: would I keep the encounter to myself and see what God would do, or would I put my faith to work (James 2:17) by telling the miraculous news to everyone who knew about the tumor?

As I think of where I had been in my walk a few years earlier, I am quite certain that, without God's preparation, I would have failed my test! God always prepares us for our test. He NEVER expects something of us that He has not already prepared us to handle! Prior to His preparation, I would have been too afraid of what people might think of me. I would have allowed someone being used by Satan --

someone who could not heal me, someone who did not know God's Word -- to steal my miracle. In Galatians 1:10, Paul confirms that we have a choice to make: please people or serve Christ. No one can do both! I am so very thankful that God had prepared me. I was sold on Jesus. Yes, it was official! I was and still am a Jesus fanatic, and I can't think of anything better to be!

"Am I now trying to win the approval of human beings, or of God? Or am I trying to please people? If I were still trying to please people, I would not be a servant of Christ" (Galatians 1:10, NIV).

I thank God that He knew when I was ready to pass the test. Did people's possible opinions and reactions cross my mind? Yes! But I did not care what anyone thought. Oh, how liberating it is when we stop trying to please people! My faith in My Father and His promises was stronger than my desire to find temporary favor with people! I knew that I had heard God's promise of healing.

I spent that day telling the few people who knew about my tumor that I was healed. I told members of the choir, my pastor, my neighbor, and others. I explained that God had said, "You are healed." But do you see the difference between what He had actually said and what I thought He said? He said, "You will not have this procedure. I will heal you," and I interpreted His words to mean, "You will not have this procedure because I will remove the tumor." "To heal" means to remove the problem -- right? Surely He had meant that I would not have to suffer any discomfort, any complications at all -- right?

I knew without doubt that God had spoken to me. I was certain that He would simply remove the tumor, and I would be healed. I would not need ANY procedure or treatment. I even called the radiologist and left a message that I would not need the UAE. That's confidence, isn't it? What a miracle it would be!

From that day in December 2001 until May 2002, I continued to believe and to claim that God had healed me. As I waited to see the manifestation with my own eyes, the radiologist, gynecologist, and I continued going through the motions. We submitted information to the insurance company to appeal the denials, and we were denied again. With each appeal I smiled, though, because I fully expected to receive approval eventually – for a procedure that I would not need! The tumor would be gone! Even as it grew, and as my abdomen swelled, I continued to claim healing. I was never in pain, and I never suffered any other symptoms.

In mid-May of 2002, I was terribly sick. For a week, my body had ached all over, and I was running a fever as high as 102 degrees. On May 19, mystified about what the problem might be, I finally decided that I needed some medicine and drove myself to an urgent care facility. After filling in the paperwork and noting that I had the flu, I was called into an examining room, where a nurse took my vitals and withdrew a blood sample from my finger. A few minutes later, though, she returned to the room looking stunned. "Honey," she said, "you don't have the flu. We don't know what's wrong with you, but you are a walking corpse!"

I thought, "I know I'm sick, but did she say 'corpse'?"

She continued, "You need to go to the hospital, and you need to get there as soon as possible."

"What's wrong with me?"

"We don't know, but whatever it is, it's very serious. Your white blood count is over 33,000, and with a normal infection it should be around 11,000! Your organs are going to start shutting down, and you need to get to the hospital quickly!"

In an effort to assess my situation properly, she then asked if I was being treated for any condition or illness. Amazingly, I told her about my tumor and the impending procedure but assured her that my current illness was not related to the tumor! Obviously, I knew very little about how dangerous even the most common ailments can be and how infections can start. She persisted, though, questioning me about any discomfort or other problems related to this tumor. I thank God that her training and knowledge of the human body led her to take the appropriate action: she phoned the on-call gynecologist from the office where I'd made an appointment, expertly filling him in about the seriousness of my condition.

The next thing I remember was arriving at the emergency entrance to the hospital, where the doctors were expecting me. I was already going in and out of consciousness, so they spoke with my husband about the tumor and decided to begin with exploratory surgery, in an attempt to determine the source of the infection. I was then wheeled into the operating room, where I told the anesthesiologist 1) that the only time I'd been put to sleep, I had been very nauseous upon waking and 2) that this tumor was not the problem because God was taking care of it! The anesthesiologist assured me that he would be prepared for the nausea – but little did I know that nausea would be the least of my concerns!

The next thirty-one days would be lost to me, and I remember nothing of them. Thus began my life-changing, near-death experience, leading to an amazing encounter with the Master!

LESSON TWO: GOD ALWAYS PREPARES YOU TO PASS THE TEST, BUT IT'S YOUR DECISION TO PASS IT!

Lesson Three

From Bad to the Worst!!!

I have been told that, after surgery and recovery, I talked to family members, but I don't remember speaking with anyone. I've also been told that I suffered agonizing pain after being moved to my hospital room. Thank God I don't remember it! Was I conscious or unconscious? How could I have responded to people and to pain, yet remember nothing? I cannot answer that question. My last memory was of speaking with the anesthesiologist before surgery.

Because of extensive damage from the tumor, which by then weighed more than twenty-two pounds, the surgery had been even more invasive than previously expected. The surgeon's knife had assaulted my body in terrible ways, and within a few hours of being assigned a room, I faced another crisis. My breathing became labored. My oxygen levels dropped. Since childhood, I had always had issues with weak lungs and bronchitis. This situation, however, was worse than bronchitis. The infection in my blood had worsened dramatically, and I was classified as septic. Sepsis alone has killed many people, but when combined with ARDS (Acute Respiratory Distress Syndrome), it is a prescription for death! As my oxygen levels plummeted, I was placed on a nasal oxygen source and then on a ventilator. I have no recollection of this frightening process.

During this phase of my journey toward healing, my son and mother took the photographs included here. These pictures were not taken by accident; rather, God had a monumental plan for them. Nothing happens by coincidence or chance. Every action is directed and guided by our loving Heavenly Father. I am deeply grateful to my family members for taking the pictures because they are recordings of a time that's lost to me. They represent my struggle at its most desperate, and without them I would have no real proof that my situation had been dire. For the many other people who have seen them, the photos are worth a thousand words! It is overwhelmingly obvious that a miracle has taken place. I am nearly dead but destined to rejoin the living. Thank you, Chad and Mama, for listening and obeying the leading of the Lord. Thank You, Lord, for prompting them to create such a visual representation of Your healing power!

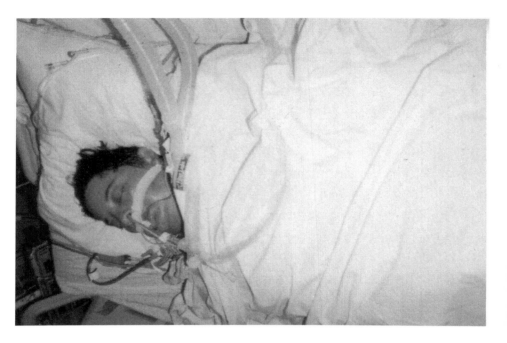

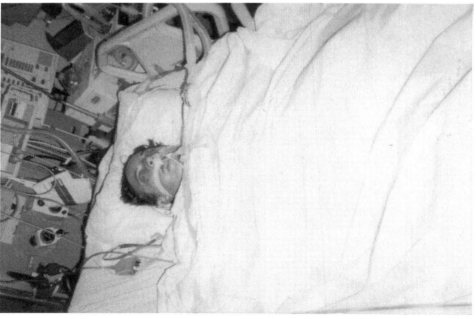

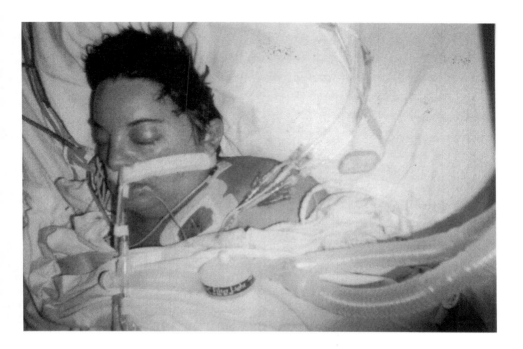

Hospital employees tried to confiscate the camera when they saw the flash, immediately assuming that the photos would be used in a future lawsuit. My mother told them, though, that "I'm taking these pictures so that, when my daughter wakes up, she will know what God has done!"

Did you hear Faith and Hope speaking? Not "if" my daughter wakes up, but "when." God heard that faith, and I know He smiled!

For my first seven days on the ventilator, intubation was through the mouth. Toward the end of the seventh day, though, as my overall health spiraled out of control, my doctors decided to perform a tracheotomy through which the ventilator would breathe for me and the chances of further infections might lessen. Nevertheless, as the doctors continued to treat the sepsis and ARDS with powerful antibiotics and every imaginable medicine, including some that had not been approved by the FDA, my body was dealt another life-threatening blow: complete renal failure. Both kidneys shut down! It was a tripod of destruction. Infection could not be removed from my body through the kidneys, and my white blood count continued to skyrocket. Stunningly, the number exceeded 66,000 – five times the norm! (As the nurse at the urgent care center had explained, with any normal infection, a person's white blood count should be around 11,000.) Additionally, my temperature was skyrocketing to 104 or even 105 degrees, and at those times I would be placed under a chill blanket in an effort to manage it. I have been told that my body would convulse from the cold external temperature as my inside temperature continued to boil. The crisis was so horrifying that my family was told, "If she survives, she will probably be in a vegetative state due to high temperatures and lack of oxygen to the brain."

As if my family needed to hear even more bad news, my oxygen levels continued to worsen, and I stopped responding to normal treatments for the Acute Respiratory Distress Syndrome. My doctors then ordered a lung biopsy to determine exactly what was happening in my lungs. However, because of the low oxygen levels, the lung could not be deflated, so a radical, or open, lung biopsy was required.

Unfortunately, the lung biopsy revealed that I also had a rare form of pneumonia known as BOOP, or Bronchiolitis Obliterans Organizing Pneumonia, which is sometimes called COP (Cryptogenic Organizing Pneumonia). According to the Mayo Clinic, COP is a rare lung condition in which the small airways (bronchioles), the tiny air-exchange sacs (alveoli), and the walls of small bronchi become inflamed and plugged with connective tissue. With the increased infection and abnormal retention of bodily fluids, my weight had ballooned from 125 pounds to more than 200. My skin actually cracked and wept fluids!

Yet even with all indicators (Sepsis, ARDS, Renal Failure, and BOOP) predicting imminent death for me, God had a plan and was completely in control. The enemy of my soul was trying with every tool at his disposal to destroy me, but no weapon could prosper enough to kill me – or to destroy my destiny!!

Countless times, the doctors told my family that I was unlikely to survive the night, but the word for prayer would be sounded like a foghorn in a storm, and the prayers of God's people would pound on the doors of heaven and carry me through. I know without doubt that God heard each heartfelt prayer, nodded His head in approval, and smiled at the continuing belief that He would save me. Never doubt that your prayers don't matter because they do! I believe that God heard those prayers and thought, "Well, if that many people are praying for my daughter Gail, maybe I can use her further in the building of my kingdom."

Two and a half weeks after the original surgery, Satan seemed to deliver the final blow to my body. Every organ, every bodily function, every sign of survival had vanished. The doctors told my family members that their worst fears had been realized. My body had crashed! I had lost all blood pressure, there was a lack of oxygen to the brain, and my heartbeat was so slow and faint that it could barely be detected.

Several dedicated and faithful visitors from my church were in the family ICU waiting room when the bad news was delivered. The doctor said, "Unfortunately, you cannot go back for the scheduled twenty-minute visitation at this time. Gail has lost all blood pressure, and there is only a barely detectable heartbeat. I hate to have to tell you this, but it will be just a matter of minutes, and her life will be over. We have tried everything, but there is no hope. We have her in the Trendelenburg position to keep blood flow to her brain, but the only thing left for you to do is pray."

And pray they did! For almost an hour, fervent prayer was delivered to Jesus in heaven, and then to the ears of the Father, by those who had kept the faith. It wouldn't be over until God said it was over! My loved ones prayed in spite of the evidence. They prayed in spite of the doctor's prognosis. They prayed in spite of the gloom that had engulfed the ICU visiting room. And then they left, but my family remained there to wait for what must inevitably be the news of my death.

A short while after those precious saints had departed from the hospital, the doctor, the same one who had delivered the terrible news of imminent death, returned and exclaimed, "We can't explain this, but Gail has strong blood pressure and a strong heartbeat. Her kidneys have started working, and she is trying to breathe on her own. It's as if someone flipped a switch!"

And of course Some One had! God had heard those prayers. He had heard and answered the prayers and proved yet again that He and He alone is in total control. It ain't over until He says it is!

When the doctors gave up and couldn't possibly explain what had happened, they themselves had to admit that the only possible answer was God's miracle! You see, God had to remove the possibility that the doctors would take credit for my recovery. Wouldn't you have loved being a fly on the wall and hearing the conversations among my doctors?

God had allowed my condition to become so grim that even the doctors were forced to realize that He had miraculously restored me. There was no other explanation! He had showed His power and majesty in a moment. As quick as the flip of a switch, every organ and every bodily function were miraculously restored. In fact, everything was working perfectly!

LESSON THREE: NEVER LOSE FAITH IN GOD'S WORD BECAUSE IT AIN'T OVER UNTIL GOD SAYS IT'S OVER!!

Lesson Four

Things UNSEEN!!!

I am fully aware that what I'm about to share with you may bring the skeptics out of the woodwork. However, I must tell you -- regardless of any repercussions, attacks, or debates from those who consider themselves too educated, intelligent, or sophisticated to believe. During the thirty-one days of my coma, of leaving my body and returning to it, I experienced numerous mysteries that I had never witnessed on this earth. I am not a sci-fi junkie whose imagination has been influenced by someone else's thoughts, dreams, or experimentation with mind-altering drugs. I have never delved into video games that introduced me to other possible realms of existence. No -- what I am relating here derives only from what I saw, heard, and experienced while my body was in the unconscious state and in the supernatural, spiritual realm. If you purchased this book and have continued to read to this point, there is undoubtedly something in you that wishes or needs to consider whether there is another realm of existence that cannot be seen with human eyes.

Boy, is there!

Because I had absolutely no comprehension of time while in the coma, I cannot tell you with any certainty how my experiences in the other realm of existence correlated with what was happening to my body in the natural realm. I know only that, at some time during the thirty-one-day coma/eternity-and-back crisis, I experienced the following events. I remind you that no one, not even the doctors, could perceive what was happening to me in the supernatural realm. The events were truly episodes unseen by human eyes, but they were also every bit as real as my body that lay in the bed, connected to a bewildering assortment of life-sustaining machines.

In what I believe to be my first experience in the supernatural realm, I was lying on a flat, cold surface, resembling granite or marble, in a white, bare room. The only other object was a medium-sized cardboard box on the floor. As my peripheral vision detected a movement, I saw a large snake exit the box and slither toward me. It approached, and its head rose up beside me to my right, so I rolled off the flat surface to my left, then steadied myself in a standing position. The creature suddenly transformed into a dark, mesh-cloud entity, but almost transparent. There were no eyes or other facial features at that moment but simply the mesh-looking cloud, yet the creature's sickening stench caused me (in my otherworldly state) to gag.

I remember a gripping fear and the nausea from the smell that had suddenly permeated the space. My eyes searched for some type of defining characteristic to determine what this "thing" might be. As I backed away from the flat surface and from the creature, I quickly scanned the interior of the space for a way to escape, all the while trying to keep an eye on the "snake." There was no evidence of a door, a window, or even a crack in the wall, however, and the creature simply hovered there, as if watching me somehow.

As I scrambled to distance myself from the creature, I backed into a wall and began feeling its texture to determine whether I might be able to punch or kick my way through it. Unfortunately, it also had the cold, solid consistency of stone, granite, or marble, so I immediately started what seemed to be a three-day search for a way out. At first I tried to search inconspicuously, but as hope dissipated, I frantically searched those walls from the floor to as high as I could reach. Then the creature started laughing a horrifyingly evil laugh. Obviously, my panicked search was amusing him.

As I've already mentioned, nothing in my personal history could have influenced this surreal experience. On the rare occasion when I've been persuaded to watch a horror movie, I've been too afraid to sit all the way through the impending attack signaled by the villain's gut-wrenching laugh – yet nothing in a movie ever competed with the maniacal laugh of the creature in my out-of-body experience. Its vibration, rather than its volume, rattled the very core of my being. The sound barrier as it's broken by a jet has nothing on the jarring disturbance of the creature's laugh!

Immediately following the terrifying laughter, a booming voice emanating from the mesh-cloud creature said, "There is no way out of here. You will never be able to escape." Then there was more laughter! As I continued to search feverishly, sweating and gasping for breath, the creature taunted me with statements obviously intended to convince me of my impending doom. It said, "No one can help you. No one can get you out because no one knows where you are, and even if anybody knew, nobody cares about you." Then it laughed its terrifying laugh again. In fact, each verbal assault was followed by a longer and louder sound-shattering, evil laugh.

At various times it would advance on me as if to engulf me in its cloud, and I would run or squat down on the floor to escape the assault. The creature seemed to have fun toying with me, probably because I had no way out, and our terrifying cat-and-mouse game lasted what felt like three days. Eventually, though, I collapsed from sheer exhaustion, sensing that my death was imminent, and whispered, "Jesus."

The next thing I remember, I was being lifted from the floor by two very strong, very loving and tender arms. The white room had gained new resplendence with a light like none I had ever seen. Most amazingly, the light seemed to encourage me to open my eyes even wider. I felt no fear, no pain.

The arms returned me gently to the marble floor, and a presence hovered above me. As I strained to see it, I could discern a semblance of some facial features, but they were enshrouded by mist. Nevertheless, I lay there calmly, serenely, my eyes adjusting to the magnificent presence, when suddenly I heard the soft and melodious voice of my Savior say, "What took you so long to call my name?"

Immediately I knew without doubt that it was Jesus! My Savior had rescued me from the enemy! As you can imagine, mere human words cannot adequately describe, convey, epitomize, or symbolize my joy or His glory!

In complete awe of His magnificence, I immediately felt drawn to repent for my self-reliant actions and independent attitude – yet what I received from Him was complete love and acceptance. I received from Him no judgment of guilt or condemnation for my flaw of self-reliance. Rather, I felt only a monumental desire to understand His question fully. Could it be that Jesus had been patiently watching and listening for my call during those three horrendous days? Had it really seemed like a long time to Him before I'd whispered His name? Was He, the Savior of the world, really so close to me that He could hear my whisper? Yes! Yes! Yes! My whisper had given Him the authority to act on my behalf. "But why did it take me so long?" I asked myself. "Why didn't I call on Him first?"

My response to Jesus was, "Lord, I am sorry. From now on, You will be my first resort, not my last."

Human nature drives us to handle life by ourselves. Think about it! We train from childhood to be independent – to work for what we want. Have you ever thought, "If it's going to be, it's up to me"? How about "If at first you don't succeed, try, try again"? Such slogans are handy reinforcements in the daily struggle to persevere, but when the battle involves the kingdom of darkness, the rules and strategies must change. Supernatural warfare requires the use of supernatural weapons.

As the Word of God tells us in Ephesians 6:12 (AMP), **"For our struggle is not against flesh and blood [contending only with physical opponents], but against the rulers, against the powers, against the world forces of** *this [present] darkness, against the spiritual forces of wickedness in the heavenly [supernatural] places."*

I hope that my experience will make you aware of the supernatural realm that is more real than the natural realm in which we operate every day. Hear me! **The kingdom of darkness is real!** It is not a dream world that someone fabricated or a virtual world that does not truly exist. The scripture above teaches us that we cannot battle our enemies with our natural strength. As with any sport, profession, or activity, all of which require proficiency, our battle with the kingdom of darkness demands that we first spend time learning the supernatural rules, practicing the supernatural procedures, and studying the supernatural strategies needed to win the supernatural war. Do not be deceived! This is not some hocus- pocus magic that we can keep up our sleeves until we're in need of an illusion! Rather, this is serious warfare. We must be in spiritual shape, have our weapons ready and in excellent operating order, and remain vigilant so that we can quickly respond to a threat. We must be armed with the Sword of the Spirit -- the powerful Word of God!

The middle of a battle is not the time to start preparing for the battle!

We know that going to war requires preparation in the natural realm and, even more so, in the spiritual. We must first invite the Holy Spirit to live within us, allowing us to discern the threats from our enemy (1 John 4:4). Next we must strengthen our faith muscle daily by hearing (and studying) the Word of God (Romans 10:17) until we believe, become saturated by, and hide in our hearts the promises of God! Then we must know how to use the name, blood, and power of Jesus, Who is The Word (John 1:1), to exercise the dominion and authority given to us so that we may be victorious over Satan.

Thank God I had the insight, knowledge, and experience necessary to realize that, at the whisper of the Name above all names, Jesus, He was my help in my time of need!

LESSON FOUR: IN TIMES OF TROUBLE, ALWAYS, ALWAYS, ALWAYS MAKE JESUS AND HIS WORD YOUR FIRST RESORT, NOT YOUR LAST!

Lesson Five

Your Enemy Is NOT a Good Sport!!!

In the previous chapter, I described what I believe was the first episode occurring in the supernatural realm during my death-and-back experience. This next incident not only allowed me the opportunity to utilize the lesson I had learned, thus convincing me that it had been the first attack by the enemy, but also provided additional lessons and insights into the supernatural realm that I will share with you.

You may be aware that, if God allows a test in your life, He will usually give you more than one opportunity to pass it. God created us, and He is completely familiar with our stubbornness or reluctance to implement a lesson learned, especially if it forces us to lose control. God is a merciful god of many chances, but the danger for us is in not knowing whether this is our first or last chance to pass the test!

We know from the Word of God (Job 1: 6-12; Luke 22:31; 1 Peter 5:8) that our enemy has to request permission from the Father to cause problems for us. We should find comfort in that strange concept because we know that the problem is part of God's plan for good and does not randomly happen, without His awareness. Did you understand what I said? Let me repeat it: every problem we face is allowed by God as part of His plan for our good!

When I first came to understand this revelation, I was immediately comforted to learn that God not only sees my pain, tears, and suffering, but also He sets limits on the extent of the enemy's attack. I realize that the concept is difficult to accept when you are in the midst of pain, anguish, or suffering, but God promises that your trouble will be used for good (Romans 8:28). Furthermore, I am not speaking from theory or a Biblical concept, but from numerous levels of experience. If I shared with you the many times that I have been attacked and afflicted by Satan, you would probably break down and cry! Just call me Josephine (a female Joseph) or Jobette (a female Job!). But I have also gained awareness from this revelation: **the size of your adversity is in direct proportion to the size of your calling!**

In response to that revelation I say, "Hallelujah! Thank You, Jesus!" So if you have experienced serious trials, troubles, circumstances, and adversities in your life, the more difficult they are or were, the more excited you should be! None of them have happened without God's awareness, filtering, and plan for use in your life.

So I was given a chance to implement the lesson learned via the previous incident. I was suddenly in a very dark and scary place. No, it was not Hell. It wasn't hot, and I heard no screams of torment and did not smell the stench of death.

As I looked around at this God-forsaken place, I encountered something resembling a jungle, but devoid of living vegetation. Instead, it consisted of shapes and formations that I had never previously seen. The atmosphere reeked of darkness and evil, and I had absolutely no idea what was about to happen, though I could sense that it was not a good place to be.

Once again, Satan appeared in the form of a snake and transformed into a dark cloud-like mesh sphere. It seemed obvious that my enemy was serious about destroying me!

He is not a good sport, and he loves to kick you when you're down! He delights in your demise.

Now let that message settle into your soul which is your mind, will, and emotions. There is no mercy in Satan. None! He has absolutely no godly traits, including compassion and kindness. Do not think you can appeal to his sympathy because he doesn't have any. Never allow yourself to think you can bargain with him. He is relentless in his pursuit of causing a rift between you and God.

You have probably heard the saying, "Give Satan an inch, and he will become your ruler." There could not be a more accurate play on words. If he gets a filthy toe into your life, he will take you down the path to destruction. That is his overall mission. It is not a game to him. He isn't playing, and you mustn't either.

Once again, Satan attempted to convince me that there was no escape, this time adding an emotional element. He would tell me, "No one cares for you. In fact, no one loves you or has ever loved you, and no one can or will even look for you." His laugh once again was villainous but somehow seemed less frightening to me even though he had company.

There were several huge, ungodly creatures with him. They had muscular, snake-like bodies with over-sized heads resembling dragons'. Long fangs protruded from their mouths, with slimy drool constantly dripping as if in anticipation of an attack. They were similar to a breeding ball of hungry anacondas but much bigger! These creatures reeked of the same stench emitted by the dark cloud-like mesh.

I am convinced that it was the stench of death from Hell itself. Even the odor of a dead animal on a hot Southern day does not replicate this wretched smell! I have a weak stomach for odors, and I cannot imagine living through all eternity in a sickening environment with such a putrid stench, in addition to all the other torments of Hell.

As I stood facing the snarling creatures and the dark mesh sphere, I was once again seeking an escape route. I know, I know. What had I learned about this plan of action from my first encounter? As is the case with mere mortals, I still thought that I could run. Run? Run where?

The dark mesh sphere would move toward me and attempt to encircle me with his darkness, and I would run in the opposite direction, only to find myself face to face with lightning-fast creatures determined to devour me. Of course, Satan was enjoying this little cat-and-mouse game of creeping up on me and causing me to run, then encouraging his creatures to attack me like a pack of ravenous dogs. After four or five repetitions of this terrifying routine, I was suddenly reminded of my "very present help in time of trouble."

This time Satan made a serious mistake. This time he said a single word that infused me with a boldness and courage beyond description. He said to me, "You cannot get away. You will spend **eternity** with me." I remember thinking, "What did he just say? Eternity with him? No way!" Mercifully, I remembered my promise to make Jesus my first resort, not my last.

With his creatures breathing the stench of death on me and Satan closing in behind me, I spun around and charged toward him with total fearlessness. His very words had reminded me of the One I belonged to and of the promise of my eternity. I remember moving quickly toward him and pointing my finger directly at him, saying, "I will not spend eternity with you because I don't belong to you. I belong to Jesus!"

As soon as I said the name of Jesus, His glory once again filled the space. I recall not only the phosphorescence of the light of His glory but also the sweet, pure fragrance of His presence. The smell of an atmosphere of purity is as overpowering to the sense of smell as the light of His glory is to the eyes. I also had an indescribable feeling of total weightlessness. It was as if I had never known any pain, adversity, trouble, care, or concern. This was the ultimate atmosphere of freedom! The removal of all care released me to experience absolute peace.

It is difficult for me to describe my experience because such a level of freedom cannot be enjoyed in this sinful world. As children, we always had concerns, even if we just wanted to get our way. Because there was always a possibility that we would be denied our want, we would feel concern, or "might not." What if we were denied?

Once I defied Satan, though, all I felt was extreme hyperbolic joy and happiness in the presence of the Lord, as well as complete freedom from an environment of sinfulness.

Prior to this mystical event, I had never realized that, no matter how well things are going in this world, there is always the weight of sin in the very atmosphere. Sin is an inherit part of our existence, and we deal with it throughout our lives. Therefore, we cannot compare this world to a sin-free environment. It's like this: even if your life is wonderful, you know that there can always be circumstances beyond your control. There is no place on Earth where you are immune to the possibility of a catastrophic event. Right? As hard as we try to prepare for, strive to prevent, and buffer ourselves from trouble, we still know that it could interfere with our plans. In the presence of Jesus, though, there is not even a thought of the **possibility** of any such occurrence. Concern is eliminated and erased from your mind, so you truly are carefree. Do you see the difference?

There is absolutely nothing that can compare with the overwhelming joy, peace, and freedom of the glory of the Lord. You will want it. You will never want to be away from it. No matter what small concessions you must make in this life in order to follow Jesus, I promise you that the result is worth the sacrifice. You will never regret the decision to receive Jesus as your Lord and Savior.

LESSON FIVE: SATAN IS RELENTLESS IN HIS ATTACKS, BUT GREATER IS HE WHO WILL ALWAYS RESCUE YOU WHEN YOU CALL HIS NAME!

Lesson Six

A Realm beyond Description!!!

The very same place that had just been dark, dreary, and void of life had become an atmosphere filled to overflowing with pure white light, purified crystal- clean air, and exuberant euphoric life, peace, and joy beyond description.

The first thing I noticed about this environment was that the white light left no space for shadows. The amazing quality of this light was that it did not cause my eyes to squint, but rather they opened wider to drink in the life-giving light. I have no idea how long I stood there, simply allowing the light to fill my complete being through eyes wide open. I could not discern the direction of the light source: I looked in front of me and to my left and right, and all I saw was pure, fulfilling light. Then I turned to my right almost 180 degrees and immediately knew that I was seeing Jesus! He was standing with His back to me, His auburn hair reaching just below His shoulders, his white robe almost lost against the pure light emanating from His glory!

I stood completely frozen in the splendor of His appearance, which truly was beyond human description. Mere words cannot adequately convey the sight, the atmosphere, or the excitement I experienced from this moment on. Seeing Him was something not of this world, something we have never witnessed in our human existence. And even if I could adequately describe it, you would not be able to comprehend it, so I must try to portray how extremely majestic His presence was.

Softly His words broke through my stupor when He said, "Take my hand, little girl. Don't be afraid." As He extended His right hand by His side, I stood wondering whether He was talking to me because He had called me "little girl."

Without moving, He seemed to beckon me to move forward toward Him. It wasn't that I was afraid; I was simply in complete and total awe of Him. Every time I hear the song *I Can Only Imagine* by MercyMe, its words ring absolutely true to my experience of being in His presence.

"Surrounded by Your glory
What will my heart feel
Will I dance for you Jesus
Or in awe of You be still
Will I stand in your presence
Or to my knees will I fall
Will I sing hallelujah
Will I be able to speak at all"

As I approached His side, I was captivated by His nail-scarred hand, opened widely, while He beaconed me to take hold of it. I can still remember the warm, loving feeling of my hand in His. Every time I recall that moment, I am brought to tears by the expression of love and caring transferred through the touching of His hand. I wanted to look up at Him, but I could not. My mind was overwhelmed by the flood of love from His touch. I just stood there in complete amazement, looking at my hand in His.

How could it be that I was holding the mighty, yet tender, right hand of the Savior? Why would the One I had come to know intimately by faith as Master of All allow a nobody like me to touch the very hand that had been nailed to the cross? Every time I attempt to tell or write about this experience, I am overwhelmed and humbled to tears. It was such a tender moment, filled with a love that I had never before experienced. As we moved forward a few steps, I finally took my eyes off His hand and looked straight out at a huge valley. We were standing on the edge of that valley. Then we began moving again, but I wasn't taking steps. Instead, I seemed to be floating above the rough rocks. This valley was filled with nothing but jagged rocks, with dead brown and gray scrub brush.

After a few seconds of our journey through the valley, Jesus said to me, "My Word says I will walk with you through the valley of the shadow of death. I will never leave you nor forsake you. Do you believe that?" Without hesitation I replied, "Oh, yes, Lord, I believe it."

Almost immediately I experienced something that I still do not understand. I was walking with Jesus as a child, but I was also still standing on the edge of that valley as an adult. I was in two places at the same time! As I replay this experience over and over in my mind, it seems to me that I was actually walking through the valley of the shadow of death while Jesus was allowing me to see Him walking with me through it. As I have pondered why He referred to me as "little girl," I have also come to realize that, no matter our age, we are always children to Him.

Having given much thought to my encounter with the Master and His words, I believe that, not only are we all children in His sight, but also his referring to me as a child was a term of endearment. In the story of the woman with the issue of hemorrhage, Jesus referred to her as "daughter."

He said to her, "Daughter, your faith has healed you. Go in peace and be freed from your suffering" (Mark 5:34 NIV).

According to the 21st Century Edition of *Strong's Exhaustive Concordance,* the Greek word that Jesus used to address this woman was a term of endearment usually reserved for a young female member of a family. Throughout the New Testament, Jesus referred to little children with Greek words that, according to the above-mentioned concordance, meant "kind regard or close relationship." After my research into this term, I am convinced that He was also speaking to me as a member of the family with kind regard and close relationship.

I recall being filled with complete trust, a child-like innocent trust, assurance, and peace as I watched what unfolded before me next. As we passed through this valley, it began to explode with colors I have never before seen, flowers so alive that they seemed to be responding to us by moving in rhythm with our movement. There was no wind, but they were all moving in complete unison, bursting with life. I have never seen a place so alive!

As we approached the far end of the valley, I saw something completely different in the distance. It sparkled like a huge diamond glistening brighter than bright sunshine reflecting on a fresh, pure white snow. It was enormous, like a planet consisting of a material more brilliant and reflective than a multi-faceted diamond! As I have pondered this scene since my experience, I have come to realize that the brilliance of the sphere was simply reflecting His brilliance!

Almost immediately upon seeing it, I realized that I was suddenly standing beside Jesus as an adult, still holding His hand. As I took in the splendor of this exquisite solitaire, reflecting and shining light beyond description, I excitedly decided that this might truly be the Kingdom of Heaven. Jesus, realizing my thoughts and anticipation, said to me, "I need you to go back. I have something for you to do." I gasped as I realized that I really was looking at Heaven! As His words settled into my thought process, I responded, "Lord, I don't want to go back." He lovingly said, "I know, but I have something important for you to do."

The next thing I recall is hearing my mother and a friend calling my name. "Gail! Gail, can you hear us? She's awake! She's awake! Call the nurse!" As I opened my eyes, a flurry of activity began to erupt around me.

I had no idea how much time had passed during this extraordinary adventure, but when I returned to my natural existence, I was electrified from the top of my head to the soles of my feet! Never before (nor since) had I felt so alive! I had been in the presence and company of the Lord Jesus, and I was ecstatically wanting to tell someone about HIM!!!

LESSON SIX: JESUS AND HEAVEN ARE VERY REAL, AND YOU ARE GOING TO LOVE THEM! PLEASE DO NOT BE DECEIVED BY TEMPORARY PLEASURE THAT CAN CAUSE YOU TO MISS IT!

Lesson Seven

It Ain't Over Until God Says So!!!

As my condition had continued to worsen day by day, even the doctors were running out of options for my treatment. They had tried every medication known to man, some not even approved by the FDA, and nothing had seemed to help. I simply spiraled downward. But God had a plan and a reason for allowing this misery to happen -- and I am so glad that He did!

Yet what's a family to do when all human hope is gone? When the relatives are told that a loved one will die or be in a vegetative state if she survives, what should family members and friends do? When the medical experts in the best hospitals in the world have been contacted for suggestions or possibilities for new treatments, and there are none, what is left for the loved ones? Simple: they must relinquish control, stop seeking human answers, and simply trust and stand on the promises of the Only One who can and will determine the outcome. It is not up to the doctors. It is not about the search for better medication. It is not about crying and pleading with God. No -- it is time for standing in complete trust and faith and for confessing that you desire His will to be done (because His will is to heal) and humbly reminding God of His Word and His promises that will move His mighty righteous hand!

There are many positive things that family and friends can do while they wait on God. They should be praying and speaking every healing scripture in the Word of God OUT LOUD in the loved one's room. They should have faith-filled music and recorded scriptures playing 24/7 in the room as an outward symbol of rebuking the enemy. There should be NO words of doubt spoken. No matter what the reports say, no matter what the facts are, the Word of God is truth, and truth changes facts! Truth changes facts!

If you fear that a visitor will speak doubt or anything contrary to the Word of God, do not allow him or her in the room. I know that such a decision seems harsh, maybe even rude, and it may gain you some criticism or persecution, but only faith-filled words must be spoken in the room. NEVER PRAY "IF" IT IS GOD'S WILL TO HEAL YOUR LOVED ONE! Think about it: "if" means that it might happen, and it might not! Such a concept represents doubt. Using "if" is a method of self-protection and indicates a lack of complete faith in God. When we speak, in faith, the promises of God, it is His reputation on the line -- not ours! It is always God's will to heal. He receives no glory when His children are sick! He receives glory when they overcome and are healed! So ask yourself why He would want them to remain sick. Obviously, He doesn't! Instead, He wants to prove His faithfulness to His Word and His power to back it up to those unbelievers who witness the miracle of His faithfulness.

You don't believe what I am telling you? Even Jesus could not heal where there was so much unbelief, not because the lack of faith limited His power but because the people of His home town were not trusting enough to bring the sick to Him because of who they knew Him to be.

Matthew 13:54-58 (KJV)

54 And when he was come into his own country, he taught them in their synagogue, insomuch that they were astonished, and said, Whence hath this man this wisdom, and these mighty works?
55 Is not this the carpenter's son? is not his mother called Mary? and his brethren, James, and Joses, and Simon, and Judas?
56 And his sisters, are they not all with us? Whence then hath this man all these things?
57 And they were offended in him. But Jesus said unto them, A prophet is not without honour, save in his own country, and in his own house.
58 And he did not many mighty works there because of their unbelief.

Matthew 13:54-58 (MSG)

53-57 When Jesus finished telling these stories, he left there, returned to his hometown, and gave a lecture in the meetinghouse. He made a real hit, impressing everyone. "We had no idea he was this good!" they said. "How did he get so wise, get such ability?" But in the next breath they were cutting him down: "We've known him since he was a kid; he's the carpenter's son. We know his mother, Mary. We know his brothers James and Joseph, Simon and Judas. All his sisters live here. Who does he think he is?" They got their noses all out of joint.
58 But Jesus said, "A prophet is taken for granted in his hometown and his family." He didn't do many miracles there because of their hostile indifference.

I love the translation of this scripture in the Message! Have you ever taken a stand on the Word and witnessed some religious people getting their noses out of joint?

Oh, boy, *I* have! I was once standing on the Word for a young man who was in a coma, and I instructed his family not to speak anything except what healing scriptures say. I told them that, by the stripes of Jesus, he was healed. As the young man's condition worsened, however, one of his seemingly religious family members came to me and said, "How dare you give this family false hope? How dare you tell them that their son is healed?" My response to her was, "I would never give a family false hope! That's why I give them the Word of God: because it is truth and real hope!" Two weeks later this young man was in rehab and working to regain his strength. I rest my case for the power of the Word of God!

In the previous scripture, we see that, even though the people in Jesus' home town knew of His miracles and powers, they could not get past His human upbringing and believe that He was the Son of God. Aren't we similar in our reluctance to believe that speaking the Word in faith brings healing? Isn't refusing to speak and stand on the Word the same as refusing to believe Who Jesus was?

John 1:1 (KJV) says, ***In the beginning was the Word, and the Word was with God, and the Word was God.***

Then John 1:14 (KJV) it continues: ***And the Word was made flesh, and dwelt among us (and we beheld his*** *glory, the glory as of the only begotten of the Father), full of grace and truth.*

So we see from these two scriptures that Jesus was the Word. We also see that He is an eternal Being, proving His pre-existence and Deity. Either you believe what the scriptures say, or you don't. There is no "sort of" believing. It's like being pregnant: either you are, or you aren't. There is no "sort of" being pregnant. If all you're willing to do is whisper the Word privately, you are not sold on believing it. If you allow what people may think about you to prevent you from speaking and standing on the Word, then you "sort of" believe it. It comes down to faith or doubt. You cannot have both. It is one or the other!

If you don't believe the Word enough to speak it in front of anybody, you don't believe the Word enough!

Refusing to speak publicly and stand on the Word of God, without reservation, is being ashamed of Jesus!

Mark 8:38 (KJV)
38 Whosoever therefore shall be ashamed of me and of my words in this adulterous and sinful generation; of him also shall the Son of man be ashamed, when he cometh in the glory of his Father with the holy angels.

Luke 9:26 (KJV)
26 For whosoever shall be ashamed of me **and of my words,** *of him shall the Son of man be ashamed, when he shall come in his own glory, and in his Father's, and of the holy angels.*

I emphasized "and of my words" to remind us that Jesus and His words are one and the same. So I repeat myself: refusing to speak publicly and stand on the Word of God, without reservation, is being ashamed of Jesus!

As I have learned, from family members and friends, of individual events and seemingly insignificant happenings during my thirty-one days of deep unconsciousness, I've become even more astounded by God's attention to this tapestry of life events. He is the master at carefully arranging friendships, relationships, and details to carry out His wonderful plan.

One such event took place a couple of nights before my big crash and the miraculous restoration. My son just happened to have a roommate who was a strong, faith-filled believer. (Of course, with God, nothing JUST HAPPENS!) With a magic marker, the roommate had just happened to write out healing scriptures on plain white paper. Those hand-written pages of powerful scriptures just happened to be brought to the hospital and just happened to be taped all the way around the bottom of my hospital bed. Can you read this account and think that the sequence of events JUST HAPPENED? No! God was showing everyone who saw the pages that He was there and that He would honor His Word! I believe with all my heart that those scriptures established around me a line of protection, while friends and family members prayed and waited for God's intervention to restore every bodily function that had been attacked and assaulted by the enemy.

Remember that things looked worse before they got better! Even after this young man's unusual act of faith, the situation continued to worsen. Satan knew that God had a plan for my life and that, if I survived, I could become a threat to his kingdom of darkness! He attacked with all that he had, but he was no match for The Word! In the natural world, those scriptures appeared to be merely words on paper. I'm sure that every person who saw them must have wondered why my condition had not improved. But God had a plan -- a plan that would eliminate all doubts about who had performed this miracle, who was truly in control, and how faithful He was to His Word. God was waiting for the perfect moment when no one could take credit for or lay claim to His glory!

Satan always turns up the heat on the situation as his last attempt to destroy all hope and faith in God. He knows that if he can plant the seed of doubt and influence words of fear and unbelief, he also can steal, kill, and destroy the environment for a miracle. But constant words of faith and prayer, announcing to the enemy and standing on the Word of God, will thwart Satan's attack and loose from the supernatural realm the healing that has already been bought and paid in full by Jesus. How can I make such a claim? Many people ask, "Isn't that just a bunch of mumbo-jumbo or wishful thinking?" I say, "No! Every word and act of faith is important to God, and His mighty right hand is moved by faith." I will explain more about it in Lesson Eight.

LESSON SEVEN: WHEN YOU BOLDLY SPEAK THE WORD OF GOD, IT'S NOT YOUR REPUTATION AT STAKE. IT'S GOD'S!

Lesson Eight

When All Human Hope is GONE!!!

Have you ever wondered why some people are healed and some are not? I know I have, and even though I will not piously tell you that I have the final answer, I do KNOW that our faith, combined with our words and actions, will move the hand of God and thus play a major role in (at the very least) some of the events surrounding a person afflicted with an illness, disease, or infirmity. But I have also learned that there are circumstances such as bitterness, resentment, anger, and the refusal to forgive that can block healing, so quickly forgive and let go of harsh feelings.

Shortly after arriving home from the hospital, I asked God that very question, and I remember His response to me vividly because it greatly altered my way of thinking about healing, faith, and hope.

As I sat on the sofa asking God the daily question of, "Lord, what's expected of me now?" I also asked, "Lord, why do some get healed and some don't?" He responded, "Do you see that electrical outlet in the wall?" I replied, "Yes, Lord." He continued, "You can't see it, but there is electricity in that outlet. When that lamp is plugged into the outlet, the bulb will work. When the plug is pulled out of the outlet, the light will not work. It's the same with healing."

"A person's faith," he said, "is the plug, and hope is the outlet. Hoping in Me is not the same thing as wishing. Hope means to expect. Wishing means that something may or may not happen. When someone hopes in Me and My Word, she expects it to happen -- no doubt, no ifs, ands, or buts -- only expectation. You see, Jesus paid at that whipping post for every healing ever needed by man, and the healing is finished in the supernatural realm, waiting for faith (the plug) to activate the hope (expectation). That's why My Word says, "By His stripes, you WERE healed." It is already done in the supernatural realm. Doubt and fear are tools of the enemy used to steal, kill, and destroy a person's healing. It is then as if the plug (faith) is pulled, and the hope (expectation) of healing is disrupted -- just as electricity stops flowing to the lamp when the plug is removed from the outlet. Many people lose faith or grow impatient and allow their words of doubt and fear to stop their healing."

Wow! Talk about a light bulb burning! What a great analogy of healing as it flows from the supernatural realm into the natural realm! I now had a much more realistic understanding of the manifestation of healing. Sometimes healing flows quickly and restoration happens suddenly, but in other circumstances the healing takes time, and therefore the plug of faith must stay plugged into the hope or expectation. For instance, after my organs were restored, I did not regain consciousness for another week. Even then, no one knew whether I would wake up or remain in a vegetative state. But God had a plan!

What a privilege it is to participate with God through faith in impacting the outcome of a situation. God doesn't

NEED our faith or participation in order to perform a miracle or to carry out His Word, but rather He allows us an opportunity to participate and to show, through trust and obedience, complete faith in Him, His Word, and His faithfulness to carry out His promises!

Hear me out. God is much smarter and more magnificent than we can comprehend. He operates on a level that we cannot fathom. Everything He does and everything He allows has a purpose and is part of a grandiose plan that we cannot see or understand.

As Isaiah 55:9 (KJV) tells us, *"For as the heavens are higher than the earth, so are my ways higher than your ways, and my thoughts than your thoughts."*

It is extremely difficult for us to see bad things, when they happen, as good things, because we haven't yet realized positive results. Traditional religion has trained us from birth that, when something bad happens, it is because God is mad and is whacking us on the head as if in a heavenly game of Whack-A-Mole. Since I have studied and learned about my Abba Father, however, I would beg to differ with that ideology.

The God Whom I have come to know through His Word has such love for us that He will allow something bad or painful to happen in order to change the path we are on or to cause us to turn to Him. I compare the situation to a parent allowing a painful vaccination to be given to his or her child in order to prevent the occurrence of a dreadful disease later. It distresses a parent to watch a child receive the shot because the child is hurting and expecting the parent to prevent the pain. The wise parent, though, recognizes that the temporary pain is preferable to the preventable disease. God will allow something painful in our lives in order to move us toward His purpose and plan for our lives, which is always a better outcome!

I can attest, from having experienced some extremely painful situations, that my words are more than a theory. They are truth! We may need time to accept the truth and to realize that it is for our good, but if we trust God, stop expecting perfection in an imperfect world, admit that we have an enemy who is relentless in his scheme to destroy us, and postpone blaming God when our lives are disappointing, we will see the truth, and it will set us free from disappointment, depression, and disillusionment.

Jesus told us in John 16:33 (KJV), ***"These things I have spoken unto you, that in me ye might have peace. In the world ye shall have tribulation: but be of good cheer; I have overcome the world."***

Jesus is encouraging us to remain patient and maintain a positive attitude in the times of trouble which are sure to come because He lives in us and has overcome the world and every situation. Furthermore, we will also overcome if we will remain in peace and trust. But will we succeed easily? NO!

Many people who are looking for an excuse to resist accepting Jesus will say things like, "If God is such a good and loving God, why does He let bad things happen to good people, to children, to those who serve Him, to… etc., etc., etc.?" Bad things happen to everyone because we live in a fallen, sinful world. God does allow things to happen that may at first seem bad, but they will always be for the good of someone.

It is up to us to decide whether to believe in and trust Him in the midst of the storm or to turn from Him and try to survive on our own. If we will simply trust that good will come from our storm, we will one day see the good. Months, years, or a lifetime may pass before we see it, but we will! It is our choice to wait and trust. If you think that you are too good for negative things to happen to you, your pride is deceiving you. If you think that this life is unfair, try existing in an environment void of God's presence, His filter, or His control. That is exactly what Hell will be, and your enemy will find tremendous joy in reminding you that you chose that place of torment and agony.

I know many people who are mad at God for bad events that have happened in their lives, and they refuse to consider that the negative experiences were in any way for someone's good. News flash! This life is not all about them and whether or not they are comfortable and happy! It is completely true that God is much more concerned about a person's character than about his or her comfort! The bad thing that happened may be for a purpose or to further the plan for another family member, for a person connected in some seemingly unrelated way, or even for the person who is now angry with God. Everything boils down to trusting God, no matter the circumstances, and believing His Word that says, in Romans 8:28 (KJV),

"And we know that in all things God works for the good of those who love him, who have been called according to his purpose."

When the above scripture says "all things," does it include bad things? YES! So if we truly trust God and His love for us, then even in bad things we will believe the Word that God will *work it for the good of those who love Him, and are part of His purpose* -- right? But part of what purpose? The purpose that is directed, influenced, or brought about because of that circumstance.

Remember: we don't know the big plan! We cannot see the end from the beginning as God can. Even if we could, we can't control it and couldn't change it! And, by the way, if it is for our good, why would we want to change it? This way of thinking is so foreign to most people because it is Kingdom thinking. I hear you asking, "What is Kingdom thinking?" It is seeing things from God's perspective. It is realizing that God's ultimate purpose is to move things, shape things, and implement things in order to move us away from the automatic pathway to Hell and into choosing to become part of His family and changing our eternal destination to Heaven.

I constantly hear people say, "I am not going to Hell because I believe in Jesus, and I know who Jesus is." Did you realize that even the demons and Satan believe in and know who Jesus is? They know that Jesus is the Messiah, they know and believe in His deity, His power, and His resurrection, yet they will never go to heaven. Why?

They will never go to heaven, first, because they are not human beings and cannot receive forgiveness or participate in God's plan for redemption, and, second (and equally important), they **know about Jesus** but do not and cannot have **an intimate relationship** with Him. Big difference! Now the question is: do you know about Jesus, or do you know Jesus intimately? More importantly, does He know you because you spend time with Him? Do you talk to Him daily? Do you read, study, and obey His Word in order to know His ways, His thoughts, His power, and most of all, His love for you?

According to Matthew 7:21-23 (NKJV), *21 "Not everyone who says to Me, 'Lord, Lord,' shall enter the kingdom of heaven, but he who does the will of My Father in heaven. 22 Many will say to Me in that day, 'Lord, Lord, have we not prophesied in Your name, cast out demons in Your name, and done many wonders in Your name?' 23 And then I will declare to them, 'I never knew you; depart from Me, you who practice lawlessness!'"*

And the same scripture in *The Message* carries the same meaning but in vastly different words: *21-23 "Knowing the correct password—saying 'Master, Master,' for instance—isn't going to get you anywhere with me. What is required is serious obedience—doing what my Father wills. I can see it now—at the Final Judgment thousands strutting up to me and saying, 'Master, we preached the Message, we bashed the demons, our God-sponsored projects had everyone talking.' And do you know what I am going to say? 'You missed the boat. All you did was use me to make yourselves important. You don't impress me one bit. You're out of here.'"*

Wow! So as we can learn from this scripture, Jesus says that entering the kingdom of heaven is conditional on doing more than simply knowing who He is, calling on His name, and doing things with selfish motives. Boom! Jesus says that we must do the will of Father God. How do we know what the Father's will is? How do we know if we are doing it? Knowing and doing are two very different things. After we determine how to be obedient to His will, the question is whether we will do it no matter the consequences.

I can tell you without reservation that, before my illness and miracle, I was a Christian of convenience. I would serve the Lord when the task fit my schedule, as long as I was not made to feel uncomfortable with my level of service, or as long as I could get lost in the crowd. You know: I was a "lukewarm" believer and therefore someone who was of little use to the Kingdom of God.

I thank God that He allowed me to go through the loss of business, loss of finances, and loss of relationships to deliver me from that lukewarm status. God knew exactly what it would take to shake me free from a comfortable, lukewarm, limited existence and to raise me to a level of boldness, commitment, and gratitude that could be used to impact this world for the Kingdom of God. I tell people that "God did not do this TO me; He allowed it FOR me!"

How can I ever thank Him enough? How can I give Him the praise, honor, and glory that He deserves? Honestly, there is no way that I can -- but He knows my heart and my desire to do so!

LESSON EIGHT: NOW IS THE TIME TO GET SERIOUS ABOUT YOUR RELATIONSHIP WITH JESUS! DO NOT PUT IT OFF FOR ONE MORE MINUTE BECAUSE YOU MAY BE JUST A HEARTBEAT FROM ETERNITY!

Lesson Nine

By His Stripes, I Am HEALED!!!

When I came into the natural realm of consciousness (as I told you at the end of Lesson Six), I was completely electrified from the top of my head to the soles of my feet. In fact, I was so filled with the glory of the Lord that I felt I would explode if I did not get the words out. It was a Saturday -- one week and one day after the crash and miraculous restoration.

Since atrophy had severely affected my muscles, I was too weak even to lift my arm so that I could scratch my nose. I was trying to speak but was still on the ventilator. As I looked around, moving only my eyes, seeing all the machines, tubes, and other medical paraphernalia, I briefly wondered what had happened to me. Yet it was much more important to tell people about Jesus! As I struggled to explain to my mama and friend about Jesus, I wondered why they couldn't read my lips. I was doing all that I could to help them understand the words that I could not speak. Later they would tell me that my lips had been barely moving, but they realized from my expression and my frustration that I was adamant about telling them something.

Finally, one of the nurses decided to bring in an ABC board from the rehabilitation department to try to determine what I was saying. My mama took hold of my hand and told me to resist when we reached the first letter, so she slid my hand, starting at A, and I resisted at J. She asked, "J?" I nodded ever so slightly. Then she placed my hand back on A, slid it until I resisted at E, and asked, "E?" Again I attempted to nod yes. When she returned my hand to A and slid it until I resisted at S, she suddenly exclaimed, "She's trying to tell us something about Jesus!" I nodded, but I wanted to scream, "Yes! Yes! Yes!"

As I continued trying to spell out what I had experienced, my body was being restored moment by moment. By Saturday evening, I had been removed from the ventilator and was asking about going to church on Sunday morning! Silly me! I had no idea how weak I really was because I felt that I could just jump right out of that bed and go. My spirit was more than willing, but my body was pitifully weak! I guess I was still feeling the effects of the glory of Jesus.

By Sunday I was telling the nurses I was hungry and begging for something to eat. I tried every trick that I could think of, including bribery, to persuade them to give me water and food. Of course, I was still on the feeding tube and had a gaping whole in my throat, as well as an open incision from the radical lung biopsy that spanned an area from under my left breast, under my arm, to my back, and almost to my left shoulder blade. I felt invincible, but, of course, in the natural world I wasn't. My body was still recovering from the attacks of multiple serious illnesses, but I was on fire for the Lord. So even though every organ was operating perfectly, I was weaker physically than I realized.

The doctor came to see me on Monday and was immediately assaulted by various nurses begging him to do something to stop my pleading and scheming for food and water. So he explained to me that I could die if food or water got into my lungs, or aspirated, through the opening in my throat. He explained that there is a process used to determine when I would be ready for food and water. It was called the "passing-the-cookie swallow test," but the reference to a cookie was so deceptive! I envisioned a chocolate chip, peanut butter, or macadamia nut cookie. Instead, it was a very dry, bland disk that tasted like dried putty. After much pleading from me, though, he was convinced to allow me a chance to pass the test on Tuesday, and he ordered that the test be administered by a respiratory therapist. I remember being nervous, excited, and determined to pass the test.

From the moment that I had awakened from the coma, I had been asking about going home. I just wanted to go to church, regardless of my pitiful weakness. Actually, I felt as if I could do anything – until the nurses got me out of the bed! As they moved me into a recliner (see picture below), I received a rude awakening. Boy, was I weak! Not only had the atrophy affected my muscles, but also I had developed a condition called foot drop, in which the muscles that allow for flexing of the ankles and toes are weakened from the patient's lying flat over an extended period of time. This condition causes the individual to drag the front of the foot when walking.

This is the picture taken just before the nurses removed the temporary feeding tube from my nose, and the respiratory therapist gave me the test.

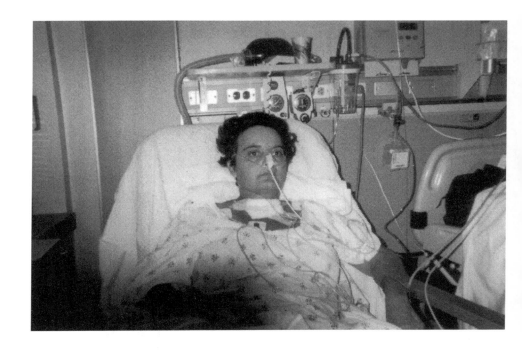

I remember praying, "Lord, help me to pass this swallow test so that I can get out of this hospital and worship You at church." And pass it I did! I ate that cookie without even the smallest cough. Then immediately following the test I again began asking – no, begging and pleading! -- for something to eat and drink.

When I learned that my first meal was on the way, I was extremely excited! I think I was envisioning something like mashed potatoes with gravy or, at worst, chicken noodle soup, but never could I have imagined pureed broccoli! Still, it was delicious! The nurse placed the plate up to my mouth, and I literally sucked that green stuff off the plate and asked for more. When she returned with another plate in her hand, she said, "I called the doctor and told him how well you did with the first serving and that you were asking for more. He said to me, 'Really? Well, when a sick baby develops his appetite, you have to feed him. Give her some more.'" That was the best food I had ever eaten -- until I was given some red Jell-o! Food had never tasted so good. None of us really know how wonderful water and food truly are until we've gone without it for several days.

My body and my short-term memory loss were being miraculously restored by God moment by moment! On Wednesday, only four days after I'd wakened, my team of doctors determined that every bodily function was working perfectly and that the only residual effect was atrophy, which I could reverse with exercise and time.

So on Wednesday afternoon I was released from the hospital to go home! Did you catch that? **Four days after a thirty-one-day coma and several terminal illnesses, I went home!** What a miracle! God exhibited His power and might in a way that I had never even considered but that no one, not even the medical professionals, could deny. Mercifully, the team of doctors who had taken such tremendous care of me were believers, and all of them acknowledged that they could take no credit for my recovery and restoration. They recognized a miracle of God!

Let me say this again: **FOUR** days after I awoke, I went home completely healed: lungs healed of ARDS and BOOP, renal failure reversed and both kidneys working perfectly, and all infection associated with sepsis gone! The only things I had to do were rebuild muscle and wait for God to restore some minor memory loss. This was quite a difference from the doctor's earlier assessments: "At best she will be in a vegetative state." "Gail has lost all blood pressure, and there is a barely detectable heart beat." "I hate to have to tell you this, but it will be just a matter of minutes, and her life will be over."

I remembered people but did have short-term memory loss and confusion relating to some places and events. Most medical professionals thought that these issues were possibly related to the strong medications that had been administered to me. Whatever the cause, though, there was nothing, NO THING, that could override the power and plan of God!

Below is the last picture taken before I left the hospital. I weighed 94 pounds at the time and had gone from 200 pounds to 94 pounds in a little over a week. Now, that is a serious weight-loss program!

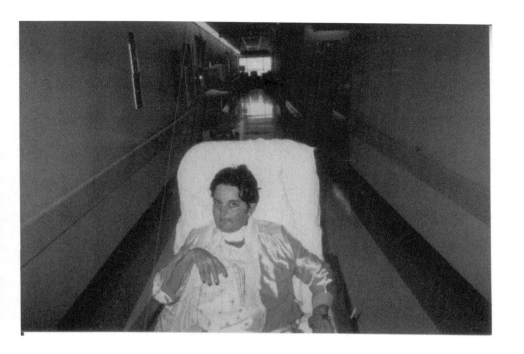

**LESSON NINE: WHAT GOD SAYS HE WILL DO,
HE WILL DO...PERFECTLY!**

Lesson Ten

OVERWHELMED!!!

Once I had arrived at home, my limitations due to atrophy became even more apparent, but I was determined. If God had restored every organ to perfection, the least I could do was work on regaining strength and muscle mass.

I was bedridden, except when I had help, for about three weeks. But with every bodily function operating perfectly, and with every fiber in me, I wanted to get up and go! When I left the hospital, I had been given a single sheet of paper describing simple exercises to do each day in order to help rebuild muscle and strength, and I was chomping at the bit to get going. When I say "simple," I mean things that we normally take for granted, such as lifting arms straight out to the sides, lifting legs while sitting in a chair, pointing and flexing toes to overcome foot drop, reaching for lightweight objects, squeezing a ball with my hands, pulling up, with help, to sit on the side of the bed, and many other everyday activities that were not only difficult but impossible for me to do during this time.

Beginning on my first day at home, I tried to consume the gravity of my miraculous healing. Even as I thanked God for the miracle, I struggled with the overwhelming question, "Why me? Why did You do this for me when so many others have been more faithful and served You more than me?"

The realization of what I had experienced was also an overwhelming sense of responsibility to know and fulfill the purpose of this miracle! In fact, it was such a concern that I could not sleep. I was consumed with understanding why the Master of all things had chosen me. If you have even a limited understanding of the power and majesty of God, I believe that you too would want to know what to do with such a miracle as I had experienced and how to proceed from that point.

Every day I prayed, "Lord, I thank You for this miracle and for the opportunity to experience all the many aspects of the supernatural realm that I was exposed to during my six-week adventure. But what do I do now? What is expected of me? Lord, I am going to pray this until I hear from You. I need to know something so that I can fulfill this overwhelming feeling of responsibility." Day after day I prayed this same prayer. God was silent.

Then, finally, on Wednesday, October 2, 2002, as I knelt by my sofa as I had done each day for almost three and a half months after coming home from the hospital, after praying that same prayer for 100-plus days, I heard God speak to me, saying, "Turn to Luke 12:48."

I could not get my Bible open quickly enough! The closest Bible to me happened to be the NIV version, and I fumbled to flip to Luke. It seemed to take me forever to find 12:48, but then there it was: *But the one who does not know and does things deserving punishment will be beaten with few blows. From everyone who has been given much, much will be demanded; and from the one who has been entrusted with much, much more will be asked.*

As I read this passage, I was more than a little confused because I was stuck on the punishment part. I thought, "Huh?" Then as I stared at this scripture, the second sentence stood out as if it were in bold print: *From everyone who has been given much, much will be demanded; and from the one who has been entrusted with much, much more will be asked.*

As I read it, I was acutely aware that I had been given so much, but I still did not have the answer to my burning question: "What do I do now?" But as I continued to read the last part of this scripture, especially the word "entrusted," I heard the Lord say to me, "I entrusted you with a miracle because I knew you would tell them it was Me." I remember thinking, "God, I know that I can always trust You, but I never thought about Your trusting me!"

I was completely in awe that God had entrusted me with a miracle. He had truly and purposefully performed a miracle in my life, not just for me but for all who would hear about it! Wow! This was confirmation that my amazing and complete restoration was not something dreamed, imagined, or fabricated. It was real, and He had now answered my prayer and given me direction.

I was to tell people about this miracle. But how should I or could I accomplish that directive? I was to share my story to let people know what God had done for a simple Southern woman who was not famous, rich, sophisticated, not even from a well-known Christian family -- a nobody

by the world's and the Christian community's standards!
My primary qualification for this miracle was that I had
been chosen to become an adopted daughter, a princess, of
the King -- and I had accepted His invitation!

**LESSON TEN: GOD DELIGHTS IN USING THE
ORDINARY TO ACHIEVE THE
EXTRAORDINARY, ULTIMATELY TO REACH A
LOST WORLD!**

Lesson Eleven

THE PROMISE!

As I was kneeling there in my family room in complete amazement and humility, I suddenly knew the purpose for my miraculous restoration and my direction forward. I replayed in my mind God's Words to me: "I entrusted you with a miracle because I knew you would tell them it was Me." My thoughts, though, immediately began to ask, "Them? Who is 'them'? How do I tell them? Will they believe me? What proof do I have?"

Then I suddenly remembered the pictures that my mama and son had taken of me in the coma. I had never even considered showing those pictures to people, especially people I did not know. I mean, let's be honest. They are not very becoming! Still, I walked into the kitchen, retrieved the pictures from the junk drawer, opened the picture folder – and realized that my unflattering pictures had become suddenly beautiful to me. As tears flowed down my cheeks, I fell in love with those pictures and decided to show them to everyone I met.

Returning to my family room and kneeling again, I said, "Lord, I make this promise to You today. I will tell this story, showing these pictures to at least one person and giving all the credit and glory to You, every day for the rest of my life on earth!" As I spoke, the weight of responsibility lifted from me, and joy and excitement filled my soul. I understood my marching orders, I knew at least part of the "something" that Jesus had for me to do, and I could hardly wait to get started telling people that God was still in the miracle business!

Unfortunately, God was not the only one who heard my promise. My enemy, Satan, heard it too! I was naïve about the extent to which he would go to prevent me from fulfilling my promise, but the attack was underway. Since that day, I have been attacked in my employment, my finances, my marriage, my family, my friendships, and many miscellaneous relationships. And as these attacks wreaked havoc in my life, I began to identify totally with Job. Nevertheless, as things grew worse and worse in my personal life, my faith and trust in God's deliverance and reversal of these circumstances grew.

I knew without a doubt that God hadn't brought me back to life from a coma, merely to be destroyed in this natural realm by the enemy from whom Jesus had rescued me. If Jesus had rescued me from the enemy then, I knew that He would rescue me now. Remember: He had told me that He had something important for me to do.

In Genesis 22:1-18, Abraham did not make decisions based on the current situation in the flesh but instead reacted in faith. He knew that God had already told him in Genesis 12: 2-3 that he and his descendants would be a great nation. In the natural, I'm sure that Abraham knew he would not become a great nation or even have descendants if he should sacrifice the promised son! He trusted God completely, knowing that if He made a promise, He would not go back on it. Abraham also knew that, even if he was required to sacrifice Isaac, God would miraculously restore the son to life. How can I be sure? Look closely at Abraham's words to his servants in Genesis 22:5 (NIV): *5 He said to his servants, "Stay here with the donkey while I and the boy go over there. We will worship and then we will come back to you."*

Do you see his faith? He said, "we will come back to you"! Abraham knew (and said) that he and Isaac would somehow return to join them! The extent of the fulfillment of this promise is described in Hebrews 11:12 (NKJV) as follows: *"12 Therefore from one man, and him as good as dead, were born as many as the stars of the sky in multitude—innumerable as the sand which is by the seashore."*

We see by this description of Abraham's descendants that God did exactly what He had promised, surpassing what Abraham probably dreamed or imagined. If God did that for Abraham, He will do it for us too!

During my times of affliction and attack by the enemy, I knew that Jesus had "something important for me to do." I knew that this was not the end. As devastating as my circumstances were, I knew that I would come through them just as I had come through every terminal illness used by the enemy against me. I also knew that I had not yet fulfilled the purpose of the miracle.

Have you ever noticed that a storm always begins and grows stronger in the middle of the ocean? It's the same with a storm in your life. If you will trust God and persevere through the storm, He will bring you through, and you will reach the other side.

I am not telling you that my struggle was easy, but nothing valuable comes easily! In spiritual warfare, victory through Jesus is guaranteed and completely worth the fight! I did not know when or how God would restore my situation, but I always trusted that He would. And He has!

I can hear you right now, saying, "But I haven't heard God speak to me." I beg to differ with you. If you have read and meditated on the Word, God has spoken to you. And the more time you spend getting to know Him and His Word, communing one-on-one with Him, you will begin to recognize His voice, as explained in John 10:27 (NKJV) and the parable of the Shepherd and His flock: ***"27 My sheep hear My voice, and I know them, and they follow Me."***

Many times I thought my situation could not get any worse, but, no matter how severe the attack, God opened doors and gave me the strength and ability to keep my promise, whether through person-to-person contact, publishing *The Shepherd's Guide of Eastern North Carolina,* preaching on the beach each summer at Emerald Isle, North Carolina, speaking at group events, sending emails, making Facebook posts, or now through the release of this book.

I made the promise, but God made the way!

LESSON ELEVEN: GOD WILL NEVER CALL YOU TO FULFILL A PURPOSE FOR WHICH HE HAS NOT ALREADY MADE PROVISIONS!

Lesson Twelve

Reason for A MIRACLE!!!

It's almost as if I can hear you asking, "Well, aren't we all going to die one day?" The answer is yes, unless Jesus comes first for God's children (one of whom I sincerely hope and pray you are), so I want you to realize that we are all always just a heartbeat from eternity! We don't know when that heartbeat will be our last because only God knows the number of days each of us has in his or her physical body. Death is part of life. Death of the physical body opens the doorway to eternity. Death is not a bad thing -- as long as you know Jesus as your personal Savior!

But did you realize that you don't have to be sick to die? Our concern should not be about dying; instead, it should be about living and fulfilling the God-given purpose for our lives. In fact, Christians should be dying of the only truly natural cause: just going to sleep and changing addresses -- to heaven!

We have been trained since birth by this world, under the control of Satan, to say, "Oh, well, we are going to die OF something." I hear people, even believers, make such statements. Did you know that when you say it, you have invited an attack by your enemy? You are giving your enemy the authority to inflict you with "something, some disease, illness, or sickness." Instead, we must learn to say what the Word of God says about us in Psalm 118:17

(NIV): *I will not die but live, and will proclaim what the Lord has done.*

Sickness is a part of the curse of sin on mankind, and Jesus paid in full for our complete healing from all disease and illness. Receiving Jesus doesn't mean that you will never be ill, but it means that you will be healed!   Either you believe that, or you don't. There is no gray area. Check it (from 1 Peter 2:24) for yourself: *24 who Himself bore our sins in His own body on the tree, that we, having died to sins, might live for righteousness—by whose stripes you were healed.*

When we read the above scripture in 1 Peter 2:24 (NKJV) which explains what Jesus did for us, there is no fine print or disclaimer saying, "This scripture is true unless you have ALS, MS, AIDS, MRSA, cancer, etc."

Even for many believers, it is almost as if they have accepted that there are certain diseases beyond the stripes of Jesus!   No! There is no affliction stronger than the blood of Jesus spilled for you at that whipping post! Let that revelation sink in, and make up your mind to believe that your healing is finished!

It amazes me that people can believe in forgiveness for their sins, but they cannot believe in their healing! In fact, it is easier to see evidence of healing than salvation. You cannot look at people and determine whether or not they are saved, but you can see that they are healed, restored, or made whole. The faith that it takes to believe either truth is the same! The faith that Jesus bought and paid for salvation is the same faith that He bought and paid for healing. He paid in full for it all!

Before we discuss the reason for a miracle, let's look at the definition of what it is. According to *Webster's New Collegiate Dictionary,* a miracle is "an extraordinary event manifesting divine intervention in human affairs." In other words, it is an event that occurs when God supernaturally overrules His own natural laws in order to affect the lives of human beings.

So why would God overrule His own laws to perform a miracle in a life? First, let's realize that miracles are not just for healing. God works miracles every day, but many are overlooked as mere coincidences. Nothing happens by coincidence: everything is either controlled by God or allowed by God for His purpose. Therefore, we know that He uses miracles to fulfill His purpose, which is always to influence people to receive His gift of eternal life through belief on Jesus Christ. *There is no other way to the kingdom of Heaven.* As Jesus said in John 14:6 (NKJV), **6 ... "I am the way, the truth, and the life. No one comes to the Father except through Me.**

Whether or not you believe that statement, it is truth! Many people are deceived into thinking that if they are "good persons," they will qualify to go to heaven. Please hear me: YOU CAN NEVER BE GOOD ENOUGH TO DESERVE HEAVEN! THE NECESSARY REQUIREMENT IS SALVATION THROUGH JESUS CHRIST!

Again, I know what you're thinking: "But, Gail, what about all those poor people in foreign countries who are Buddhists, Muslims, Hindus, etc., or have no religion at all and have not heard about Jesus?"

First, God is a merciful God, and He knows what He is doing. He would never hold someone accountable for something that he or she had never been told. Instead, he holds people accountable for the lives they led, based on what they knew.

Second, you should be concerned about your life -- accepting Jesus as your Lord, repenting for your sins, and giving those poor people in foreign countries the opportunity to hear about the Good News that they can receive forgiveness for their sins and have life eternal in heaven through believing on Jesus!

Many people want to argue various points in an effort to avoid the real issue: addressing their own salvation! Others want to believe but aren't convinced that the Word is true. A man recently told me that Jesus eliminated the Old Testament, so the New Testament automatically gave everyone salvation! FALSE! Salvation is available to everyone, but it is not automatic, and Jesus did not eliminate the Old Testament. In fact, as Jesus said in Matthew 5:17(AMP), ***"Do not think that I came to do away with or undo the Law [of Moses] or the [writings of the] Prophets; I did not come to destroy but to fulfill."*** See? The Law and the Prophets are the Old Testament!

To prove that salvation is not automatic, we simply need to refer to the words of Jesus in John 3:16 (AMP): ***"For God*** *so [greatly] loved and dearly prized the world, that He [even] gave His [One and] only begotten Son, so that whoever believes and trusts in Him [as Savior] shall not perish, but have eternal life."* We see in this Scripture that anyone (whoever) can be saved, but he or she must "believe and trust in Him" to receive the gift of eternal life!

So why are there two testaments?

This is the simplest way that I can explain the concept: all of us have heard of a Last Will and Testament. It is a legal document explaining how and to whom the belongings of a deceased person are to be distributed. Well, the Old Testament was God's legal document explaining how and what the Jewish people would receive, based on His will. It also explained how they would receive forgiveness of their sins through the sacrifice of animals administered by God-appointed priests.

When Jesus came and died for the sins of mankind, God revised His Testament to include you and me! He simplified it for our good! No longer were animal sacrifices necessary to cover our sins because Jesus was the perfect Sacrifice, and anyone who believed on Him would be forgiven and adopted into God's family. He or she would receive life eternal! No longer did anyone need a priest to go before God in the Holy of Holies because Jesus became the High Priest interceding on our behalf. No longer was the family of God only for those of Jewish heritage. Anyone could be adopted by God!

So, you see, the Old Testament was a foreshadowing of God's ultimate Testament -- to fulfill His will of expanding His family and including all of mankind. Therefore, Jesus did not change God's Law or His Word in the Prophets but rather condensed it into one commandment that covers it all in Matthew 22:37-40 (NKJV): *Jesus said to him, "'You shall love the Lord your God with all your heart, with all your soul, and with all your mind.' This is the first and great commandment. 39 And the second is like it: 'You shall love your neighbor as yourself.' 40 On these two commandments hang all the Law and the Prophets."*

I don't know about you, but thinking of the Old and New Testaments in this way makes it simple for me to comprehend. As with any instruction books, both Testaments give us the details on how to fulfill the above Great Commandment with stories and information that helps us understand how much God loves us, what His will is for us, and how we can acquire the abundant life Jesus died to give us here on earth and for eternity. The concept is really rather simple. The hard part is living it out when we have been accustomed to living life so differently. We must learn to overcome our selfish nature and deal with an enemy that is determined to destroy us!

Jesus confirmed this reality in John 10:10 (AMP), saying, *"The thief comes only in order to steal and kill and destroy. I came that they may have and enjoy life, and have it in abundance [to the full, till it overflows].*

So I said all of that to answer the original question: why would God overrule His own laws to perform a miracle in a life, especially in a life of someone ordinary like me? Or you?

God uses miracles to show mankind that He is God! He made the laws of nature that operate in this world, and only He can supersede them. His purpose is to get our attention, to cause people to turn from their sinful natures, and to realize that He is real, that He is Who He says He is, and that He loves them with such an unconditional love that He allowed His Son to die a horrible death so that many may become His children -- part of His royal family -- and live a life of perfection for all eternity!

LESSON TWELVE: NEVER HAS ANYONE LOVED YOU OR *WILL* ANYONE LOVE YOU THE WAY GOD DOES! TO BE ADOPTED INTO HIS FAMILY, TURN THE PAGE AND SPEAK THIS SINNER'S PRAYER!

THE SINNER'S PRAYER

If, after reading my story, you decide that you need to receive Jesus as your Lord and Savior, simply SPEAK this prayer in faith and allow Jesus to enter your heart.

Heavenly Father, I come to You in the Name of Jesus and ask You to forgive my sin and receive me into Your family. In accordance with Your Word that says if I call on the name of the Lord, confess with my mouth that Jesus is Lord, and believe in my heart that You raised Him from the dead, I will be saved. So today, in faith, I believe Your Word and confess with my mouth that Jesus is Lord and that You raised Him from the dead. Thank You Lord for coming into my heart, for giving me life eternal, and for being Lord over my life. AMEN!

If you prayed this prayer, the next and very important step, is to find a body of believers (church) where the Word of God is being preached and taught. You need to hear the Word of God and to be with like-minded people because there is strength in numbers. Why do you need strength?

Your enemy (Satan) wants nothing more than to steal, kill, and destroy your gift of abundant life received through Jesus Christ. Do not be deceived! Without allowing the

Word to develop your strong foundation, you will be easy prey for Satan's lies and deception. Many people have never been told about this scheme of the devil and therefore, never live the victorious life God intended for them to live on earth.

I pray that as you read this, you make the decision that you want all that God has promised to you as His child. As you hear and read the Word of God those promises are revealed to you and you will be favored and blessed in ways you never dreamed or imagined!